PARKS FOR THE PEOPLE

How FREDERICK LAW OLMSTED Designed America

BY
Elizabeth Partridge

ART BY
Becca Stadtlander

VIKING

VIKING

An imprint of Penguin Random House LLC, New York

First published in the United States of America by Viking,

an imprint of Penguin Random House LLC, 2022

Visit us online at penguinrandomhouse.com.

Library of Congress Cataloging-in-Publication Data is available.

Manufactured in China

ISBN 9781984835154

1   3   5   7   9   10   8   6   4   2

HH

Book design by Jim Hoover   Typeset in Australis Pro, Bernhard Fashion Std, TPTC CW Book Italic, and Winery JNL

The illustrations in this book were created by watercolor and gouache

This is a work of nonfiction. Some names and identifying details have been changed.

To my four Wild Ones,
happiest in gardens and parks and forests:
Lila, Oliver, Ezra, and Ruben. −E. P.

For Paul. −B. S.

**N**obody could get Frederick Law Olmsted to sit still. He thought memorizing obscure facts and learning ancient languages was boring. He fiddled and squirmed and stared out the window, longing to be outside.

After school, Fred raced through town. He visited his father's dry goods store and checked in on the blacksmith and carriage maker.

There was always plenty going on in Fred's town of Hartford,

Connecticut. Like the rest of America in the 1830s, it was growing fast. Immigrants arrived every day by wagon and riverboat. Nearby factories turned out clocks and glass bottles, and power looms clattered in the cotton mills.

The rush and clamor of town soon wore Fred out. He headed for the nearby woods. He waded through streams, climbed trees, and threw himself down in sweet-smelling meadows to rest. Out in the woods, he felt calm and free.

As soon as Fred turned fifteen he went to work as a surveyor's apprentice. He tramped over hills and around lakes. For his job, he learned to read a compass, measure distances, and draw maps. Sometimes Fred got restless and bored and sketched in his notebook.

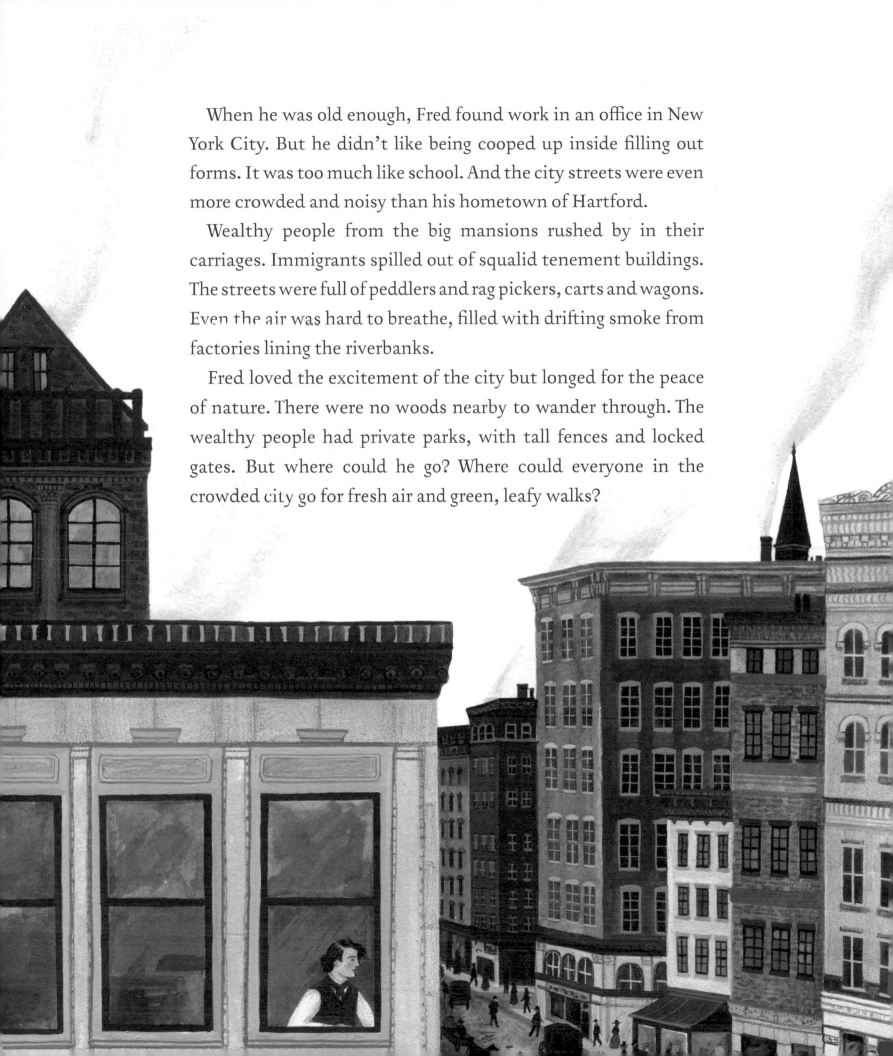

When he was old enough, Fred found work in an office in New York City. But he didn't like being cooped up inside filling out forms. It was too much like school. And the city streets were even more crowded and noisy than his hometown of Hartford.

Wealthy people from the big mansions rushed by in their carriages. Immigrants spilled out of squalid tenement buildings. The streets were full of peddlers and rag pickers, carts and wagons. Even the air was hard to breathe, filled with drifting smoke from factories lining the riverbanks.

Fred loved the excitement of the city but longed for the peace of nature. There were no woods nearby to wander through. The wealthy people had private parks, with tall fences and locked gates. But where could he go? Where could everyone in the crowded city go for fresh air and green, leafy walks?

In the evenings, Fred and his friends talked late into the night about what kind of country the still-new America would become. How could the United States accommodate the thousands of immigrants arriving every year? What about all the farm families moving to the cities, looking for work in the factories? How could the country stay together as the North and the South bitterly disagreed over slavery?

Fred was eager to do something that would help answer these big questions. Something important, not just filling out papers. But he didn't know what. He tried farming, first in one place then another. After a few years he left his farm, and traveled through the South and Texas, writing about what he saw. But he was restless and unsettled.

By the fall of 1857, Fred was thirty-five years old and he still had not found a way to make a difference to America. He was also dead broke. He owed money to his father, his friends, even the man who stabled his horse.

Doing something important would have to wait. Right now, he needed to pay his bills.

Fred found work supervising several thousand men clearing land in Manhattan to make into a park. It didn't seem like an important job to Fred, but it was all he could find. Besides, as he wrote to his brother John, "What else can I do for a living?"

Every morning Fred got up early and organized his crews of Irish and German immigrants willing to work long, hard days for low pay. The men drained swamps, cut down thickets, and tore down old shacks.

Several small villages dotted the landscape. The largest was Seneca Village, where most of the property was owned by African Americans. The residents were proud of their town. They had built

three churches for worship, graveyards to bury their dead, and a school to educate their children.

To make way for the park, the city government said everyone would have to sell their property to the city. The residents hired lawyers and fought hard in the courts to retain their land, but they lost. They would have to move out when construction began on the park.

The city held a contest to pick the best design to turn the cleared land into a park. Fred's friend, architect Calvert Vaux, asked Fred to work with him on a plan. *Now* Fred was excited. This was his chance to bring the peace of nature to the big city. Using the skills he had learned as a surveyor's apprentice in Hartford, Fred was full of ideas on how to make a park for "the poor and rich, the young and the old."

Fred and Calvert worked feverishly up to the very last minute
the day the plans were due. It was after midnight when they
finally rushed in their plans.

Fred and Calvert's design won!

Fred was put in charge of building the park. Along with his new wife and three stepchildren, Fred moved into an empty convent left standing on the cleared land. He led his workers in blasting out rocks, and building paths, roads, bridges, and arches. He had hundreds of thousands of trees and shrubs planted.

Central Park opened in the winter of 1858, though work on the park

would continue for years. From day one, it was full of visitors. There were no high fences, no locked gates. The workmen who built the park and the poorest immigrants from the tenements were as welcome as the wealthy people from the big houses. It was "the first real park made in this country," Fred wrote to a friend, "a democratic development of the highest significance."

Fred was proud of his work. He had created common ground for everyone in New York City.

But just as Central Park was coming together, the United States was falling apart. Southern states seceded from the Union and the Civil War began. Fred was determined that the young new democracy of the United States needed to be preserved, and slavery needed to end. He rushed down to the nation's capital, Washington, DC, eager to help.

Fred was shocked to see the state of the troops. Thousands of soldiers were in the capital, injured and sick, poorly fed and clothed. Morale was terrible. Twenty kitchens hastily set up in the basement of the Capitol Building turned out loaves of bread, trying to provide enough food for the hungry men.

Fred did everything he could to improve medical care for the Union soldiers in his new position as Executive Secretary of the US Sanitary Commission. A worried friend noticed that Fred worked "with a steady, feverish intensity till four in the morning, sleeps on a sofa in his clothes, and breakfasts on *strong coffee and pickles*!!!"

It was a chaotic, divisive time, and many of Fred's ideas were ignored. He got more and more frustrated. Finally, he quit.

Gold Rush fever was running high since the discovery of gold on the West Coast a few years earlier, and now it hit Fred as well. In 1863 he and his family moved to the foothills of California, where Fred took a job running a gold mining company.

Gold seekers were everywhere, panning for gold, digging shafts, tearing up the riverbeds with hydraulic equipment.

Even on the smallest trails Fred saw "empty sardine boxes, meat, oyster and fruit cans, wine, ale, olive and sauce bottles, with playing cards and torn leaves of novels." He hated to see the mess left behind by the greedy fortune hunters. This was no way to treat America's wilderness.

In the crushing heat of summer, Fred and his family took a trip into the high Sierras. Using pack mules and horses, they followed steep trails into the cool Yosemite Valley and camped at the foot of a spectacular waterfall. Fred was awed by the giant Sequoia trees stretching to the sky, the rushing, tumbling water, and the sheer granite cliffs.

Fred and his family were some of the first white people to camp in Yosemite Valley. The Ahwahneechee had lived there for thousands of years, but a few years earlier they had been violently driven out by a posse of white men, their houses burned down and food supplies destroyed.

When Fred was asked to join a new commission to plan for the future of Yosemite, he jumped at the chance. He knew there were already men eager to build a sawmill in the valley to cut down the ancient trees and make them into lumber. He wanted Yosemite to be set aside "for the free enjoyment of the people" before it was too late. Just as he'd seen Hartford

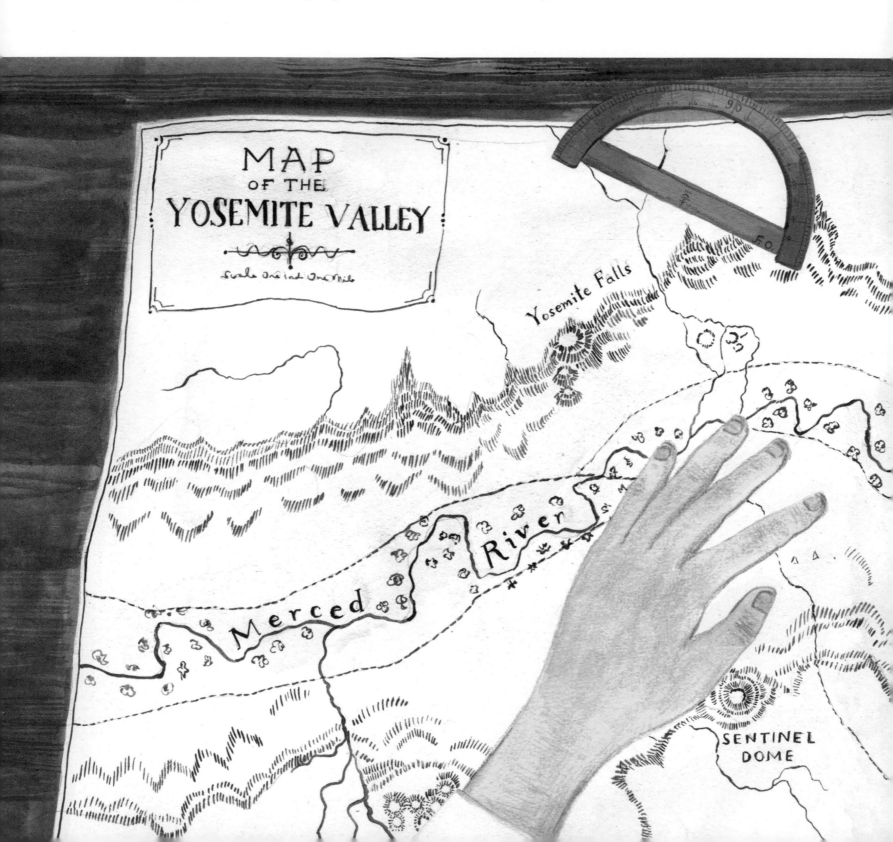

and New York City fill with new arrivals from Europe, he knew more people—*many* more—would come to California.

Fred hired surveyors to map Yosemite. He wrote up a lengthy report of his vision for the valley and presented his ideas to the rest of the commissioners.

On April 9th, 1865, telegraph lines to California carried news of the Union Army's victory. The United States would remain united! But just six days later came word that President Lincoln had been assassinated. He was mourned in newspapers across the country. Like so many others, Fred was devastated. Lincoln, responsible for keeping the country together, was dead. The work to begin healing the country had not even begun.

More bad news followed. Fred was told that the gold mine would be shut down. He was out of work and would need to start all over again.

Yosemite would become one of the first national parks in the United States, but Fred couldn't stay in California to help. He returned to New York City and teamed up with Calvert Vaux again to design Prospect Park in Brooklyn.

It wasn't just Brooklyn. Cities across America wanted their own parks. And they wanted Fred to design them.

Fred rode trains and stagecoaches and carriages to Boston and Atlanta and Chicago and San Francisco. He trampled through scrub brush and woodlands, waded across boggy marshlands, and climbed over rough rocky hills. He kept going every day until he was exhausted.

At night he stayed up late, writing proposals and letters by lamplight. Fred was eager to create as many parks as he could, as fast as he could. Making peaceful, leafy places for everyone was his way to make a difference to America. He even had a name for what he did: landscape architecture.

But no matter how hard he worked, he could not possibly design parks for every city.

Then in 1874 Fred was asked to design the grounds of the United States Capitol.

He walked the rough, uneven ground under stunted trees struggling to grow in the heavy clay soil. Washington, DC, was very different from the last time Fred had been there. The soldiers were long gone, the kitchens in the basement of the Capitol Building removed. Inside were the Supreme Court, Congress, and the Library of Congress. Outside, rutted roads and dusty footpaths crisscrossed the grounds.

Fred got to work doing what he did best. He had cartloads of fertilizer added to the barren soil. He had roads and paths graded, old trees removed, and new ones brought in.

It wasn't always easy. Thieves snuck in at night and stole hundreds of the new plantings. A herd of cattle escaped onto the grounds, trampling bushes and tearing tender new leaves off the trees. Newspapers printed scathing reviews as the work progressed. But Fred never gave up.

Next came work on the Capitol building itself. Fred thought it looked unsettled and precarious where it sat on the top of a small hill. He had marble terraces built on three sides. Wide stairs led to a new, stately entrance. Lamps lit the plaza at night.

It was a bold, ambitious design. The Capitol building stood in the middle of a beautiful park. Pathways curved through the trees, and long diagonal drives gave visitors an inspiring view of the Capitol dome. A summerhouse on the West Front Lawn offered a cool, restful place.

Rich and poor, old and young, citizen and immigrant, everyone was welcome. Fred felt it was the most important work he had ever done. Here, at last, he had created common ground for all of America.

Author's Note

Frederick Law Olmsted designed college and university grounds, suburbs, private gardens, and arboretums. His projects included widely different challenges like the National Zoo in Washington, DC, the Chicago World's Fair, and the Biltmore Estate in Asheville, North Carolina.

But his most visionary works are his parks. Deeply interested in bringing the benefits of the outdoors to people in cities, he wanted everyone to enjoy the parks together. It was not only good for each individual, it was good for democracy. And with an uncanny awareness of the huge population increases in the country, he worked passionately to preserve the natural, wild beauty of Yosemite and Niagara Falls before it was too late.

Some of Olmsted's parks were built where no one lived, but some had rich human stories going on just before the parks were created, like Seneca Village and the Yosemite Valley. Ironically, Olmsted's commitment to preserving and creating open land didn't extend to protecting the communities of people living on that land, many of whom were Black, Indigenous, or poor whites.

CENTRAL PARK AND SENECA VILLAGE

Seneca Village was a settlement of more than two hundred people on about five acres between 82nd and 89th Streets, and Seventh and Eighth Avenues in Manhattan. About two-thirds of the residents were free Blacks, and the rest mostly Irish and German immigrants. Many of the Black villagers owned their property, and if it was worth $250, that ownership gave male property owners the right to vote. (No women were allowed to vote until 1920.) This was unusual at a time when slavery still flourished in the South and had not been completely outlawed in New York State, which didn't happen until 1827, just thirty-one years before Central Park opened.

Using the right of eminent domain, New York City bought the villagers' property, whether they wanted to sell or not. Eminent domain allows governments to purchase private property for public use. Some villagers felt they were being paid too little and fought in court to see if they could get a higher price. So far, historians have not found any letters, newspaper articles, or oral histories that would let us know how Olmsted felt about the destruction of Seneca Village.

YOSEMITE NATIONAL PARK & THE AHWAHNEECHEE

For several thousand years the Ahwahneechee, a subtribe of the Mono-Paiute, lived in Yosemite Valley. Every year they burnt off the underbrush and young pine trees. This left

Yosemite Valley with meadows where deer and rabbits grazed and the Ahwahneechee hunted. The fires also kept fast-growing pines from overshadowing the oak trees that provided acorns, a staple of their diet.

Just months after California became a state in 1850, a small group of white men tried to capture the Ahwahneechee and bring them to a nearby reservation, but the Ahwahneechee ran away into the steep surrounding mountains. The battalion burned their houses and food caches, hoping to starve them out. For the next few years the Ahwahneechee resisted, but soon they were rounded up and forced onto the reservation. By the time Olmsted visited Yosemite for the first time, the Ahwahneechee were no longer living in the valley.

Today there is a small reconstructed Ahwahneechee village in Yosemite Valley that is used by local tribal members for ceremonies and other special occasions.

Until I began research for this book, I didn't realize how Frederick Law Olmsted's work has touched me throughout my life.

When I was young, my parents used to take us on long camping trips in Yosemite. We rented mules to carry our equipment and hiked through mountain passes and along streams. My dad shared with me his love of Yosemite, the fresh, sweet smells, and the millions of stars in the velvety night sky.

As I dug deep into research for this book,

it opened up an old tender spot as well. Until I was in third grade, we lived on ten acres in a Northern California valley, surrounded by a huge cattle ranch. We had oak trees to climb, a creek to wade in, and horses to ride.

As the nearby towns grew larger, more water was needed for everybody to drink, wash, and fill their swimming pools. Like in Seneca Village, the government used the power of eminent domain to pay us for our ten acres and force us to leave. Heavy construction equipment dammed off one end of our valley. The creek water rose, and our valley became a reservoir.

We moved to the city, which was full of cars and noise and people. My classroom was on the second floor of a big school with loud bells and hundreds of kids. I spent my days staring out the window, daydreaming about oak trees and streams.

As an adult, I still live in that same city. It's more full of cars and noise and people than ever before. I always have a dog—or two—and get out for a walk in a park almost every day.

There is a beautiful spot nearby where I like to take the dogs, Mountain View Cemetery. It feels like a park, with wide curving paths, tall trees, and gently sloping hills. My grandparents are buried there, and my parents. Back in the 1880s, a forward-thinking relative bought a large family plot. To my surprise, I discovered Olmsted had designed the cemetery while he was in California. When my time comes, I'll be buried here too, to rest forever in the peaceful, shady place Olmsted created.

Olmsted in 1850 at age 28.

1822 Born April 26 in Hartford, Connecticut.

1825 Younger brother John Hull Olmsted born.

1828 Visits Niagara Falls.

1837–1839 Works as a surveyor's apprentice.

1840 Works as a clerk in New York City. Sees crowded living conditions on Lower East Side.

1843–1857 Works various jobs, including sailor, farmer, writer, and reporter. Travels through American South, Texas, and Europe.

1857 Returns to NYC and takes job supervising men clearing land that will become Central Park.
   Brother John dies.

1858 Wins design contest for Central Park with Calvert Vaux.

1859 On June 13, marries his deceased brother John's widow, Mary Perkins Olmsted. Adopts their three children, Owen, Charlotte, and John.

1861 Moves to Washington, DC, and heads up US Sanitary Commission, improving medical care for Union troops.
   Daughter Marion born.

1863 Moves to California. Manages gold mining company in foothills not far from Yosemite.

1822 US made up of twenty-four states, stretching westward from the Atlantic Ocean.

1825 Erie Canal opens, connecting Atlantic Ocean and Great Lakes.

1830s First railroads built in US.

1837 Telegraph invented.

1840 90 percent of all Americans live in rural areas. Most are farmers.

1847 More than 50,000 Irish immigrants arrive in New York City, fleeing starvation in the Great Irish Famine.

1853 Most of present-day Arizona and New Mexico bought from Mexico for $15 million.

1859 Abraham Lincoln elected president.

1861–1865 Civil War between North and South.

1865 Submits report on Yosemite Valley to .... **1865** The North wins the Civil War. President
California State Legislature. Unable to find Lincoln is assassinated.
enough work in California, heads back to New York
City with his family later in the year.

1866 Works on Prospect Park in Brooklyn with
Calvert Vaux.

1868 Designs Delaware Park, part of the Buffalo
Park System in New York, with Vaux. **1869** First transcontinental railroad completed,
largely replaces stagecoach lines and wagon trains.

1870 Son Henry Perkins Olmsted born. (At age
seven, officially renamed Frederick Law Olmsted Jr.)

1871 Designs Jackson Park, part of the South .... **1871** The Great Chicago Fire leaves 90,000 homeless.
Park System in Chicago, Illinois, with Vaux. **1872** Yellowstone National Park established as the
1872 Partnership with Vaux ends amiably. United States' first national park.
1873 Blue jeans patented, called "Copper Riveted
Overalls"

1874 Submits plans for US Capitol Grounds as well
as for Mount Royal Park, Montreal, Canada.

1886 Statue of Liberty dedicated October 28.

1878 Submits plans for what will become Emerald
Necklace park system in Boston.

1879 Moves to Brookline, Massachusetts. .... **1879** Thomas Edison tests his first light bulb.

1887 Works with Vaux again to design Niagara Falls.

1890 Redesigns Jackson Park for upcoming .... **1890** Wounded Knee Massacre, South Dakota.
Chicago World's Fair, opening in 1893.   US population has increased by 25 percent in last
decade, largely due to immigration.

1891 Designs Cherokee Park, part of Louisville
Park System. **1892** Ellis Island Immigration Station opens.

1895 Retires. Sons Frederick Law Olmsted Jr.
and John Olmsted take over business. **1896** Utah enters Union, bringing total number
of states to forty-five.

1903 Dies August 28.

1906 Yosemite Valley and the Mariposa Grove
become Yosemite National Park, country's third
national park.

Sources, Resources, & Bibliography

"... what else can I ..."

"Frederick Law Olmsted Papers: Correspondence, 1838–1928; General Correspondence, 1838–1928; 1857, July–Dec.," Library of Congress, Washington, DC 20540 USA, image 53, accessed November 8, 2019, loc.gov/item/mss351210047/.

Frederick Law Olmsted to John Hull Olmsted, September 11, 1857. Frederick Law Olmsted papers, Manuscript Division, Library of Congress, Washington, DC.

"... the poor and the rich ..."

Justin Martin, *Genius of Place: The Life of Frederick Law Olmsted* (Cambridge, MA: Da Capo Press, 2011), 140.

"... with a steady ..."

Frederick Law Olmsted and Jane Turner Censer, *Defending the Union: The Civil War and the US Sanitary Commission, 1861–1863* (Baltimore: Johns Hopkins University Press, 1986), 108.

"... empty sardine boxes ..."

Frederick Law Olmsted and Charles E. Beveridge, *Frederick Law Olmsted: Writings on Landscape, Culture, and Society* (New York: Literary Classics of the United States, 2015), 355.

"... for the free ..."

"Yosemite and the Mariposa Grove: A Preliminary Report, 1865. By Frederick Law Olmsted," accessed July 20, 2019, yosemite.ca.us/library/olmsted/report.html.

FULL LENGTH BIOGRAPHIES:

Laura Wood Roper, *FLO: A Biography of Frederick Law Olmsted* (Baltimore: Johns Hopkins, 1973).

Witold Rybczynski, *A Clearing in the Distance: Frederick Law Olmsted and America in the Nineteenth Century* (New York: Scribner, 1999).

ONLINE SOURCES:

Frederick Law Olmsted Papers, Digital Collections, Library of Congress, accessed September 30, 2019, loc.gov/collections/frederick-law-olmsted-papers/about-this-collection/.

Frederick Law Olmsted National Historic Site, US National Park Service, accessed November 8, 2019, nps.gov/frla/index.htm.

Seneca Village, New York City, US National Park Service, accessed November 8, 2019, nps.gov/articles/seneca-village-new-york-city.htm.

Yosemite National Park, US National Park Service, accessed November 8, 2019, nps.gov/yose/index.htm. Includes information about the Ahwahneechee, nps.gov/yose/learn/historyculture/yosemite-indians.htm.

"US Capitol Grounds," Architect of the Capitol, accessed November 8, 2019, aoc.gov/explore-capitol-campus/buildings-grounds.